DIESELS in the West Midlands and central Wales

1Z51

DIESELS
IN THE WEST MIDLANDS AND CENTRAL WALES

GEOFFREY F. BANNISTER

D. BRADFORD BARTON LIMITED

Frontispiece: A steady Welsh drizzle and a greasy rail makes climbing difficult as spotlight-fitted Class 37 No. 37 192 slogs up towards Llangunllo summit on the Central Wales line with an excursion from Weston-super-Mare to Shrewsbury on 1 September 1974.

ISBN 0 85153 218 7
printed in Great Britain by H. E. Warne Ltd, London and St. Austell
for the publishers

D. BRADFORD BARTON LTD · Trethellan House · Truro · Cornwall · England

introduction

'Steam Obituary, 3rd March 1967' read the headline in one of the leading West Midland evening newspapers. 'Can diesel locomotives ever be photogenic? demanded another writer in a railway periodical of the same month.

Eight years have elapsed since that epic day in 1967 when regular steam traction ceased both in the West Midlands and Central Wales. The Jonahs and the pessimists had their say and cameras were put away but the very fact that this present volume is in print is testimony to the continued and unabated interest in all things rail, created among young and old alike.

Although the photographs within this volume cover the period from 1962 to 1974, the accent is firmly placed on the enormous changes and sequence of events which have modified the railway landscape almost beyond recognition, both aesthetically and materially in terms of actual mileage. A multitude of signal boxes, station complexes and sidings, not to mention motive power depots, have literally disappeared from the scene in a very short space of time, replaced perhaps by some re-development scheme or more likely by 'forests' of rose bay willow herb.

The photographs contained herein have been selected to illustrate both normal and unusual train working in the region. Less variety and more uniformity in motive power classes has been tempered with illustrations of special workings for the interest of the reader.

Ten years ago, thought of preserving an L.M.S. Class '5' or a G.W.R. 'Hall' appeared mildly amusing; ten years hence, thoughts of preserving a Class 47 will raise no eyebrows.

With the exception of those captioned otherwise, all photographs are by the writer.

Bathed in evening sunshine, Class 24 No. 24 030 and 24 074 with the 18.15 Bescot to Shrewsbury (Coton Hill) Class 8 freight pass Wolverhampton on the through goods line. On the right an EMU has just arrived from Manchester while at the adjacent platform stands the DMU service to Wellington and Shrewsbury, 8 August 1974.

One of the Derby Research Centre's own locomotives heads a special Tribometer test train at Wolverhampton (High Level) on 6 October 1972. The train consists of Class 23 'Baby Deltic' No. 5901, a laboratory coach (BSK 975046 VB), the Tribometer vehicle (COV-AB 99900 through piped) and a stores van (BSO 975036 VB).

The south end of Wolverhampton (Low Level) station on 11 May 1970 with the arrival of the 17.48 single DMU from Birmingham (Snow Hill). At this date Low Level was undergoing conversion to a parcels concentration depot. Through services from Paddington to Birkenhead ceased in March 1967. The local Birmingham service terminated on 6 March 1972.

Wolverhampton (Low Level) fully converted to a parcels depot. Class 25 No. 25 212 is about to leave with a parcels train for Derby on 7 August 1974. The only access available is by spur to the former Midland line at Heath Town Junction.

A special train of long welded rail crosses Oxley Viaduct on 19 July 1973 hauled by Class 40 No. 217 *Carinthia.* This train is from Hookagate long welded rail depot (Shrewsbury) and is bound for Old Oak Common. Electrification over this short section of the old G.W.R. route to Chester is necessary to facilitate empty stock working from Oxley carriage sidings to High Level (now simply named Wolverhampton).

Once known as Birches and Bilbrook Halt, Bilbrook station is roused by the passage of the one remaining through express service from London (Euston), the 17.45 to Shrewsbury. The locomotive in charge is an unidentified Class 47.

Derailment of the 09.20 Bescot to Shrewsbury (Coton Hill) freight on 19 August 1974 entailed additional duties for two Immingham-based Class 47s. The train engine is No. 47 365 whilst No. 47 367 is in charge of the Bescot steam crane, having lifted a derailed wagon following removal of its wheels.

Codsall station on the final day of 1970 with a Waterston to Albion train of Gulf oil tank wagons double-headed by Class 37s Nos. 6943 and 6972, showing an incorrect reporting number. Due to engineering work at Brettell Lane on the Stourbridge Junction to Priestfield direct line, these trains were, at the time, diverted via Craven Arms and Salop.

Climbing the 1 in 150 Shifnal bank towards Madeley Junction on 23 August 1973, the 09.45 Wellingborough to Croes Newydd (for Brymbo steel works) iron ore train is hauled by Class 45 No. 68 *Royal Fusilier* with brake tenders. Class 47 No. 1824, with an M.G.R. coal train from Ironbridge power station, is standing in the down refuge siding.

A string of coal empties from Ironbridge (CEGB) to Silverdale approaches Cosford with a 'visiting' Class 50 No. 408 on 8 August 1973. These workings were normally the preserve of Class 47s fitted with slow speed control.

An interior view in Cosford signal box, built just prior to World War II to cater for traffic to and from the RAF station here, shows signalman Ken Butler awaiting the passage of an Ironbridge (CEGB) to Daw Mill empty M.G.R. train.

On 11 August 1972, English Electric Class 50 No. 425 takes the Lightmoor Junction single line at Madeley Junction in charge of a coal train en route from Silverdale (Stoke) to Ironbridge power station. This class is rarely seen in this vicinity.

rush' Class 47 No.1904 on a Littleton Colliery to Ironbridge coal train passing through Shifnal station. This now much modified, with platform awnings removed but with G.W.R seats and repainted passenger notice maining.

Empty stock from the Royal Train returning from Welshpool to Wolverton following overnight occupation by H.R.H. Prince Charles on 23 May 1974. The short train comprises ex-L.N.W.R. power brake Nos .5154, Stanier saloons Nos. 45006 and 45005, plus BFK 5155. The locomotives are Nos. 25 072 and 25 068.

During the summer months, Sunday traffic over the ex-G.W.R. Wolverhampton to Salop line is supplemented by various specials. Depicted here is a Long Eaton to Barmouth 'mystery' excursion traversing the 'wrong line' at Albrighton. This train, hauled by No. 40 022 *Laconia* will run over the Abbey Foregate loop at Shrewsbury, thus eliminating reversal.

Two Class 24s (Nos. 24 079 and 24 083) working in tandem, head another Sunday 'mystery', on this occasion from Alfreton to Barmouth, over the up line between Albrighton and Cosford owing to engineering works blocking the down. The P.W. gang in the foreground appear to be experiencing difficulty with rail alignment.

Wellington, in Shropshire, once a rail centre of some importance, forms the background to Class 47 No. 1817 as it runs off the now-truncated and singled line from Stafford with an M.G.R. coal train for Ironbridge loaded at Granville Colliery – now the terminal point of this erstwhile rail link between the two towns. This trip necessitates reversal in Wellington station and at Madeley Junction. Passenger service between Wellington and Stafford was withdrawn on 7 September 1964.

Major modifications at Wellington are visible in this scene looking towards Shrewsbury, with a charter train arriving from Stirling on 10 August 1974 with No. 47 191 in charge. Points of interest are the site of the former Wellington shed (right) and the ex-G.W.R. Much Wenlock branch bay platform as well as the ex-L.N.W.R. Coalport bay.

The 09.23 Manchester (Piccadilly) to Penzance express awaits departure from Shrewsbury with Class 47 No.47 140 at the head, a view taken from the prison road, which shows Abbey Foregate, and the river Severn beneath the station. This express, routed via Hereford and Bristol, is a Saturdays-only summer working.

Class 40 No. 40 004 entering Shrewsbury station with a northbound ballast train of 'Sea Lion' wagons from the Hereford line, July 1974.

Having previously reversed a parcels train into Platform 1, now used exclusively for traffic of this nature, English Electric Class 37 No. 37 207 'gets the road' for Coton Hill sidings. Crewe Junction signal box, by the curve, figured in the mysterious high speed derailment of the night West of England mail here on 15 October 1907.

Indicative of the service of earlier years, Class 47 No. 47 234 has been substituted for t basic DMU service from Crewe to Cardiff (via Hereford), and is about to leave with hi speed Mark II stock. The DMU in the bay is for the Central Wales line.

SHREWSBURY
6Z14

Class 47 No. 1814, with the 12.30 Littleton Colliery to Ironbridge M.G.R. train of slack, passing the derelict stone-built goods shed at Madeley Court in April 1970. The building of a second CEGB power station at Ironbridge on the site of Buildwas station has resulted in the single line Madeley Junction to Lightmoor Junction branch carrying more traffic than ever before.

Class 24 No. 5061 struggles up the bank from Coalbrookdale towards Lightmoor Junction on 1 April 1970 with a train of empty tanks from Ironbridge to Ellesmere Port. The double track section from Lightmoor to the power station at Buildwas has been retained and worked as up and down through sidings.

End of track at Buildwas, Ironbridge, CEGB power station, as Class 47 No. 1814 arrives with a coal train from West Cannock Colliery on 2 April 1970. The train is on the refurbished section of the Severn Valley line and is seen prior to the locomotive detaching and running round. The hopper wagons are then drawn through the coal discharge plant at $\frac{1}{2}$ mph, all locomotives being fitted with slow speed control for this purpose.

A rural scene in the middle of Telford New Town, with an Ironbridge to Silverdale (Stoke) empty coal train just north of Madeley Court with Class 47 350 in charge, 1 August 1974.

Ironbridge power station headshunt with Class 47 No. 1818 on an M.G.R. coal train from the Cannock Chase coalfield. This is the sole remaining portion of the Severn Valley line (except for the preserved Bridgnorth to Bewdley section); April 1970.

Class 24 No. 5137 and Class 08 diesel shunter No. 3397 with an out-of-gauge load from the Horsehay Ironworks bound for Motherwell, consisting of two crane girders, approaching the level crossing at Dawley Parva, Telford, on 2 September 1971. This short section of the former G.W.R. Ketley Junction to Lightmoor Junction branch was retained after closure for occasional use—usually about once a month—to transport steel products, such as these two crane girders from the Ironworks.

An excursion from Swansea to a north-western destination traverses the Grand Junction line at Portobello Crossing, Wolverhampton, hauled by Class 47 No. 47 097 *Thor.* The photograph is taken from the site of the Portobello Shunt Frame signal box, demolished the previous month or so to the date of this photograph in the derailment of an oil train.

The pit banks and mining subsidence hollows filled with water remind the passing traveller of the 'Black Country's' industrial heritage as No. 47 052 heads a Sunday excursion along the Grand Junction line near Willenhall, Wolverhampton, on 30 June 1974.

One of the original ten Class 44 'Peaks', formerly D8 but now No. 44 005 *Cross Fell,* leaves Bescot down marshalling yard with a Class 8 freight for the north-east, travelling via Walsall, Ryecroft Junction and Lichfield City. These early Derby Sulzer 'Peaks' are based in the Nottingham Division and are rarely seen in the West Midlands other than working freights in and out of Bescot.

Class 40 No. 40 181 brings a trip freight off the Walsall line into Bescot marshalling yard, surrounded by miscellaneous ironmongery. The reporting number 9 T 32 is the Bescot 'trip' number for local freight between Wednesbury or Ocker Hill, Hednesford, Birchills and Bloxwich.

The 04.27 Stoke yard to St. Blazey 'clayliner' empties, with Class 52 diesel-hydraulic No. 1049 *Western Monarch* in charge, leaving the east end of Bescot yard on 13 February 1974. This train will reach W.R. territory via Perry Barr, Galton Junction, Stourbridge and Hartlebury and is one of the few diesel hydraulic turns regularly to penetrate the L.M. Region since takeover in 1965. These 'clayliner' trains are electric hauled between Stoke and Bescot.

lass 45 No. 92 pushing
cavalcade of four
lass 47s and a Class
at the depot at
escot after leaving
e refuelling line.

A Sunday 'mystery excursion' from Wellingborough to Barmouth threads the heart of the industrial Black Country between Tipton and Coseley on 8 September 1974. The train engine is No. 47 201.

D 3839

The 09.40 Edinburgh to Bristol express hauled by Class 47 050 passing Barnt Green station—junction for Redditch and the truncated ex-M.R. Ashchurch branch.

‹-L.M.S.R. diesel-
ectric shunter D3839
; station pilot at the
d 'New Street'
irmingham in the
ımmer of 1962. The
N.W.R. signal
mained until the
ation was rebuilt
ome few years later.
[Gregory, Wolverhampton]

EE Class 40 D377 resting after its long journey from Glasgow with the daytime Glasgow to Birmingham (New Street) express. A steam-hauled evening commuter train is leaving the adjacent bay platform; July 1962. [Gregory, Wolverhampton]

D 5013 brings empty coaching stock into Birmingham (New Street) during July 1962. The decrepit L.N.W.R. signal box obscures the site of the present Birmingham Power box. [Gregory, Wolverhampton]

A feature of 1974 was the number of Western Region Class 52 diesel-hydraulics working into Birmingham (New Street) on Paddington trains. On 24 May No.1068 *Western Reliance,* having brought in the 09.25 from Paddington to Platform 1, prepares to run round.

An Ironbridge to Silverdale empty stock train sets back on to the Bushbury spur at Cannock Road Junction prior to the locomotive (Class 47 No.1839) running round, 8 August 1972. This view northwards shows the former G.W. Wolverhampton to Shrewsbury main line curving left towards Stafford Road Junction, the cleared ground formerly the site of Stafford Road shed coaling stage. On the right, the Bushbury spur connects with the ex-L.N.W.R. Grand Junction line—always used by the Royal Train on Queen Victoria's journeys from Osborne or Windsor to Scotland.

The end of the Bushbury spur connecting the former G.W. line from Cannock Road Junction to the L.N.W. Grand Junction line. Class 47 No. 1683 with an empty slack train from Ironbridge to Littleton Colliery waits at the junction while Class 25 No. 7602 wheels an Etruria to Wednesbury coal train along the Grand Junction line.

Chipman Chemical Company No. 2 weed killing train at Priestfield Junction working over the former G.W.R. Birmingham to Wolverhampton line on 10 June 1971. The train is made up of Class 25 No. 5266, two brake vans, four 45-ton tankers, machinery van (ex-S.R. composite brake) and mess van (ex-S.R. third open brake). On the right is the lifted Oxford, Worcester & Wolverhampton Railway line to Dudley.

Run-down of a main line! The 17.10 single-unit DMU from Birmingham (Snow Hill) to Wolverhampton (Low Level) pauses hopefully at Swan Village between West Bromwich and Wednesbury on 20 March 1971. Closure took place twelve months later, the section between Wednesbury and Swan Village being still retained as a siding.

A Teesport to Wednesbury oil train, headed by Class 45 No. 99 *3rd Carabinier* arrives at the site of Wednesbury (ex-L.N.W.R.) station on 9 February 1974. Passenger services between Dudley and Walsall were withdrawn ten years earlier, although one platform still remains here.

Class 20s in tandem; Nos. 20 177 and 20 090 pass Stourbridge Junction with a northbound freight for Bescot in June 1974. The Class 47 in the adjacent loop beyond the signal box is waiting to give banking assistance through Brettell Lane and up to Dudley.

Class 24 No. 7621, having taken a trip freight to Pensnett, runs south from Kingswinford Junction towards the holding sidings at Stourbridge Junction on 23 February 1974. The Kingswinford Junction to Oxley (Wolverhampton) branch was truncated first at Baggeridge Junction, then later cut back to Pensnett after closure in 1965.

The present terminus of the former Kingswinford Junction to Oxley branch line is at a coal concentration yard immediately north of the site of Pensnett Halt. This view is towards Gornal Halt and the now-lifted section in the direction of Baggeridge Junction. Class 25 No. 5273 is leaving for Kingswinford Junction, 2 March 1974, with the coal yard 0-4-0D alongside.

The 10.30 Worcester to Birmingham (New Street), running via Stourbridge and Galton Junction, approaches dilapidated Cradley Heath station on the Stourbridge Extension line, 4 September 1974. This is now the only locomotive-hauled train regularly booked over this line on a passenger turn. In this case, it is somewhat unusually headed by a W.R. Class 31 instead of the more customary Class 25.

Norton Bridge, on the former Western Division main line of the L.M.S.R., is the junction for Stoke-on-Trent. Here the 08.45 (Saturday only) Liverpool to Penzance, hauled by No. 47 332, occupies the up slow line. Note the somewhat unusual appendage of a Syke's Banner repeater signal to the sophisticated colour light signalling complex.

Class 40 No. 212 *Aureol* heading a rake of empty coaching stock from Crewe to Vauxhall (Birmingham) near Cranberry on 16 June 1973.

A north-bound freightliner train of Chrysler car components behind No. 47 265 heads over the ex-L.N.W.R. electrified main line near Mill Meece, between Norton Bridge and Crewe, August 1974.

One of the class that once was the mainstay of L.M. Region diesel motive power on main line express duties, Class 40 No. 231 heads 'The Merseyside Express' over the northern approaches to Stafford. The line diverging to the west is the former L.N.W.R. branch to Wellington and that to the east the ex-G.N.R. line to Uttoxeter and Derby.

The 10.20 Euston to Liverpool (Lime Street), with Class 47 No. 1982 towing E3197 and train, rounds the curve from Queensville past Stafford No.1 signal box (now demolished). The electric locomotive is in tow due to Sunday engineering work between Rugeley and Stafford in the winter of 1973.

An unidentified Type 4 locomotive eases an express round Queensville curve south of Stafford during the early years of diesel electric haulage. The signal box is of typical L.N.W.R. deslgn. [Gregory, Wolverhampton]

The ill-fated English Electric diesel D P 2 speeds the down 'Mid-day Scot' around the same curve. This locomotive was the test bed design for the later Class 50s and was entrusted with many important duties including the haulage of the West Coast T.P.O.

[Gregory, Wolverhampton]

P.W. engineers have full occupation of the Wolverhampton to Stafford line on Sunday 13 May 1973 for track renewal between Fordhouses and Penkridge. Class 47 No. 1583 is at the head of a prefabricated track train. Blockage of this line necessitates diversions of trains to and from Birmingham over the Trent Valley route and thence via Cannock and Walsall.

A specially equipped Football League Charter Train—complete with blacked-out discotheque coach at the front—from Oldham to Pokesdown (Bournemouth) passing the site of the wartime platform and sidings of Featherstone ordnance depot, on the Grand Junction line, north-west of Wolverhampton hauled by Class 47 No. 1690, April 1973.

Royal Train empty stock passing the Goodyear Factory at Bushbury, Wolverhampton, en route from Manchester to Oxford on 22 May 1974. On the previous evening the Prince of Wales had attended a function in Manchester and was travelling from Euston. The two engines are Nos. 25 072 and 25 068, the vehicles in the train being Power brake No. 5154; Saloon No. 45006 (Kitchen); Saloon No. 45005 (Lounge); Saloon No. 2901 (Attendants' Compartment) and BFK No. 5155.

The 10.36 Manchester (Piccadilly) to Euston comes to a stand at Bushbury Junction, Wolverhampton, to detach Class 50 No. 437 from train engine Class 86 No. E3128 on Sunday 29 October 1972. Engineering operations on the Trent Valley line and also between Stafford and Norton Bridge involved diesel haulage between Crewe and Wolverhampton.

Servicing overhead line equipment between Stafford and Rugeley on the Trent Valley line on Sundays in March 1972, necessitated diesel haulage of Euston-bound trains with their electric locomotives in tow. Class 47 No. 1820 enjoys a change from 'merry-go-round' coal operation, leading Class 85 E 3093 and the 07.46 Holyhead to Euston into Rugeley (TV) station.

On 31 March 1974, No. 47 335 with 86 034 and 08.52 Liverpool (Lime Street) to Euston lays a smoke screen over Rugeley as it gets away from Brereton Sidings signal box after being checked there by a previous train. This diversionary route over Cannock Chase is frequently used when Sunday engineering works affect the Trent Valley line.

Unusual motive power for a passenger train over Cannock Chase on Sunday, 24 February 1974 has Class 37 No. 6827 with a Class 86 electric and a diverted Liverpool (Lime Street) to Euston train, slogging up the gradient on full throttle through the closed Rugeley Town station. This Class 37 was currently based at Saltley for crew training purposes.

EE Class 50 No. 432 passes Brereton Sidings box at Rugeley, with a Liverpool to Birmingham train diverted over the Rugeley to Walsall freight line in February 1974. The box formerly controlled the junction with the mineral line—now lifted—to Brereton Colliery, and today controls movement of traffic into Rugeley CEGB power station.

Approaching the site of Brindley Heath station, Cannock Chase, on Sunday 31 March 1974, is the diverted 07.57 Holyhead to Euston with No. 47 095 towing No. 86 220 with pantograph lowered. Brindley Heath station was closed in April 1959 but passenger services between Rugeley and Walsall were not finally withdrawn until January 1965.

With the waste tips of West Cannock Colliery dominating the sky line, a Manchester to Euston express speeds south behind No. 47 441, towing No. 86 221 between Rugeley and Hednesford in March 1974.

Passing Hednesford No. 3 signal box on the former L.N.W.R. Rugeley–Cannock–Walsall line—now closed to regular passenger trains—the 08.24 Liverpool (Lime Street) to Euston is headed by Class 47 No. 1721 on 11 July 1971. The junction here serves West Cannock Colliery to the left; the L.N.W.R. signals have now been replaced by BR upper quadrants.

The 10.00 Liverpool (Lime Street) to Euston diverted express passing Hednesford No. 1 box on a Sunday in February 1974, with a Class 47 towing No. 86 223. Following closure of No. 2 box in 1973, No. 1 now controls the junction of the branch to Cannock Wood Colliery.

Closed but not forgotten! Hednesford station on 10 March 1974, as a diverted Euston to Manchester (Piccadilly) train comes through behind Class 47 No. 47 448. Although the Walsall to Rugeley line has been closed to passengers for some years, occasional excursions have commenced their journey here, for example some to Blackpool Illuminations in October 1974.

On 28 January 1973, Class 45 No. 11 heads a diverted Leeds to Penzance express past Ryecroft Junction at Walsall. This train has run via Lichfield (City) and Bescot because of engineering works on the normal route through Tamworth. The crew are exercising caution in passing Class 25 No. 5277 with the Bescot crane which is engaged in 'mopping up' duties following a derailment here earlier in the week.

The same train leaving the Lichfield line, in a setting that shows the four lines coverging at Ryecroft. These are the ex-L.N.W.R. routes from Lichfield to Dudley, and from Rugeley, as well as the two ex-Midland Railway spurs from that company's line—now lifted—from Sutton Coldfield to Wolverhampton.

Pleck Junction (formerly Bescot East) is the divergence point from the Walsall to Dudley line for traffic going north or south by virtue of two spurs. Class 46 No. 46 050, with a Birmingham to Leeds (diverted) train is coming off the south spur from Bescot station en route to regain its normal path at Wichnor Junction.

Another diversion with the 10.20 Birmingham to Leeds at Rushall Crossing near Walsall, in the charge of Class 45 No. 27. The ex-L.N.W.R. signal box, although still retaining Webb block telegraph for boxes to the east, is equipped with a 'fringe' train describer for use in conjunction with the power box at Walsall.

Class 45 No.44 at speed with a Leeds express past Fossway Crossing signal box on 11 February 1973. The box is of a design common to many of the L.N.W.R. structures in the West Midlands, and is of interest in that permissive block working was allowed to enable trains to proceed under caution when shunting was in progress near Anglesea Sidings, the next block post. This accounts for the call-on arm on the home signal. Automatic barriers were installed here later in 1973 and the signal box closed.

A diverted Sunday Birmingham to Leeds train hauled by Class 45 No. 24 leaving Lichfield City station on 4 August 1974, having travelled via Bescot and Ryecroft Junction, Walsall.

Although rebuilt in strictly functional style, Tamworth (High Level) station still boasted a pair of original cast-iron notices at the north end of the platform in February 1973. Class 45 No. 57 heads the 12.30 Leeds to Bristol. Remains of the connecting spur to the TV line can be seen on the left.

Class 45 130 ambles northwards along the O.W.W.R. with a trip freight from Stourbridge Junction, 6 September 1974. The cleared site on the right is the remains of the former G.W.R. Stourbridge Junction shed.

The empty Stoke Yard to St. Blazey 'clayliner' passing Stourbridge Junction on 9 February 1974, with Class 52 diesel-hydraulic No. 1069 *Western Vanguard* making a rare appearance on London Midland Region metals.

Class 25 187 with the 10.30 Worcester to Birmingham takes the Stourbridge Extension line at Stourbridge North Junction on 6 September 1974. The O.W.W.R. continues towards Dudley on the right.

Class 45 No. 123 with a Bescot to Bristol freight accelerates past Hartlebury signal box in February 1973 over the former Oxford, Worcester & Wolverhampton Railway, now the boundary between Western and London Midland regions.

Class 47 No. 1691 with a trip freight from Kidderminster to Elmley Lovett Sidings (for RAF Hartlebury) enters Hartlebury station on 20 February 1973. Formerly the junction for Bewdley and the Severn Valley line, this now serves Stourport power station only.

The 07.24 Bristol to Newcastle, hauled by Class 46 No. 46 020, about to take the junction for Stoke Works and Birmingham (now singled) at Droitwich Spa in February 1973. A Western Region D C E special train, headed by a Class 31, waits in the up loop.

Class 25 No. 5188, still in green livery, about to leave Droitwich Spa station at the head of the 10.30 Worcester to Birmingham local. This particular service runs via Kidderminster, Stourbridge Junction and Galton Junction.

Class 35 'Hymek' No. 7026 enters Worcester Shrub Hill from the refuelling depot preparatory to working the 13.40 to Paddington, 7 January 1974.

Class 47 No. 1630 with a Weston-super-Mare to Leeds train passing Norton Junction near Worcester in June 1973, using the spur from Abbotswood Junction, which connects the former Midland Railway Birmingham to Gloucester main line with the now singled O.W.W.R. to Evesham and Oxford (left).

Class 31 No. 31 309 trundles a south-bound ballast train along the former Midland line from Birmingham to Gloucester, near Wadborough in February 1974. The locomotive's reporting number has obviously not been changed since a previous trip with a Crewe to Gloucester parcels.

Two of the resident Lickey banking engines at Bromsgrove in June 1971 were 'Hymek' Class 35 Nos. 7022 and 7021, seen here assisting a Severn Tunnel Junction to Washwood Heath Class 8 freight up the incline to Blackwell.

Rare motive power tackling the two miles of continuous 1 in 37 Lickey Bank between Bromsgrove and Blackwell, on 26 June 1971; Class 52 No. 1060 *Western Dominic* has an easy task with the nine-coach load the 09.40 Bristol (Temple Meads) to Derby. No. 1060 worked through to New Street, returning later with a train for Paignton.

IM52

Another banking combination on Lickey; No. 37 294 and No. 25 029, having crossed over to the down line, coast through Bromsgrove station to the holding sidings, after assisting a north-bound freight up to Blackwell; 13 July 1974.

Over the Paddington to Worcester line on 2 June 1973, the only 'Hymek' diesel-hydraulic working was the 16.15 Worcester to Paddington, seen here arriving at Evesham. Most of the '35s' had been displaced on these diagrams by Class 31/2 or Class 47 diesel-electrics and the ten 'Hymek' survivors latterly were confined to freight workings.

No. 1021 *Western Cavalier* heads southwards through Blakedown with empty clay wagons from Stoke to St. Blazey on 16 February 1974. For some months from October 1973, Class 52s were diagrammed regularly to work this train from W.R. into L.M. region territory as far as Bescot from whence electric haulage was used. From April 1974, Laira-based Class 46s began to take over these duties.

The 13.20 test train from Crewe (CM & EE Dept) to Church Stretton approaching Sutton Bridge Junction, Shrewsbury, on 9 August 1973, hauled by Class 47 No.1894 in immaculate ex-works condition.

The 09.25 Manchester to Penzance (SO), headed by Class 47 No. 1744, passing Sutton Bridge Junction on 21 July 1974. Since 1973, Class 47s have had a virtual monopoly of summer express passenger workings over the north-west line but the number of passenger trains working over this route in summer was radically reduced when rationalisation of workings through Birmingham (New Street) was introduced.

No. 37 186 leans to the curve between Marshbrook and Little Stretton with an unusually-routed excursion from Swindon to Blackpool. The incorrect reporting number, together with late running, suggests a probable engine failure earlier in the day; 26 October 1974.

Soccer special; a Manchester United supporters' train en route for Cardiff approaches Sutton Bridge Ground Frame at Shrewsbury on a Saturday in August 1974, hauled by Class 47 No. 47 280.

One of the named Class 47s, No.47 083 *Orion,* with the 10.15 Paignton to Manchester (Piccadilly) approaches Dorrington, between Church Stretton and Shrewsbury, on 29 June 1974.

1J01

The 11.05 freight from Grange Junction Sidings to Radyr, drifts down the bank through Church Stretton station on 17 August 1973 with Class 45 No. 45 107 in charge.

ıother CM and EE Test Train from Crewe to Church Stretton 'running in' with Class 47 No. 1916, passing former ›rrington station in August 1973. The station here has now been converted into a private residence and the Unigate ·eamery, formerly the source of a daily milk train to London, now uses road transport.

Class 46 No. 144 heads south through Church Stretton with a freight for Severn Tunnel Junction in August 1972. The Shrewsbury & Hereford signal box still contains an L.N.W.R. lever frame and stands opposite the original station buildings, replaced just prior to World War I by a new G.W.R.-L.N.W.R. Joint line structure south of the overbridge from which the photograph was taken.

A charter train running from Paddington to Shrewsbury, via Swansea, traversed the scenic Central Wales line on Sunday 1 September 1974, and is seen here crossing Knucklas Viaduct over the Heyop Valley, headed by No. 37 169.

The 08.45 Newquay to Manchester (Piccadilly) approaching the attractively sited Marshbrook Crossing on the Shrewsbury and Hereford line on 29 June 1974 with Class 47 No. 47 140 in charge.

On the Shrewsbury and Hereford (ex-L.N.W.-G.W. Joint line) the 08.35 RWS (registered wagon service) from Carlisle to Severn Tunnel Junction, hauled by No. 47 123, passes the site of Stretford Bridge Junction, just north of Craven Arms, 27 July 1974. The ill-fated Bishops Castle Railway turned away left here towards Plowden and Lydham Heath.

The 12.40 Motorail from St. Austell to Crewe approaching Craven Arms Crossing signal box on 29 June 1974, hauled by one of the Class 47s.

Another of the very many Class 47s—No. 47 087 *Cyclops*—drifting down the grade towards Craven Arms on the same day with a train-load of salt from Middlewich in Cheshire bound for Baglan Bay near Briton Ferry.

No. 37 206, with a southbound engineers' train of 'Grampus' wagons, is just inside Western Region territory as it heads towards Craven Arms station on a July Saturday in 1974.

The 11.40 Paignton to Manchester hauled by Class 45 No. 15 heads north past the abandoned Ludlow racecourse platform at Bromfield on a warm Saturday in June 1972.

Two views on the former Shrewsbury and Welshpool G.W.-L.M.S. Joint line at Meole Brace, Shrewsbury, once the site of exchange sidings with the Shropshire & Montgomeryshire Light Railway. Above, the 09.40 (SO) Euston to Aberystwyth, hauled by Class 24 Nos. 24 134 and 24 092, gets to grips with the climb up from Sutton Bridge Junction and (below) Nos. 24 085 and 24 123, running in tandem, pass the site of the exchange sidings, with a train from Aberystwyth, 20 July 1974. The down line from Sutton Bridge to Hookagate had recently been taken out of use, with an extended single line token used from Sutton Bridge to Westbury.

Two Class 24s (Nos. 24 085 and 24 053) bring a special charter train from Aberystwyth to Euston into Westbury in May 1974. The station is now a private house, passenger services being withdrawn in 1960; the signal box here controls a level crossing and passing loop, the only block post between Welshpool and Shrewsbury.

Standard motive power on the ex-Cambrian main line; No. 25 145 and No. 24 062 bring the 10.07 Aberystwyth to Euston ïnto Caersws station fifty minutes late on 7 September 1974 due to storm force 10 gales over Wales causing fallen trees, structural damage and flooding at Dovey Junction.

Class 24 Nos. 5050 and 5146 coast down the 1 in 95 past the site of Breidden station between Westbury and Welshpool on 30 June 1973, with a day excursion from Brighton to Aberystwyth.

Earlier on the same day these two locomotives battled with the gradient, this time with the 10.05 from Aberystwyth to Euston, and are seen on the climb towards Westbury from Buttington.

On 6 July 1974, No. 40171 and No. 24 087 provided an unusual combination of motive power over the ex-Cambrian line, passing Buttington Crossing near Welshpool with the down Euston to Aberystwyth express.

An up express from Aberystwyth storms up Breidden bank past the site of the former Plas-y-Court Halt towards Westbury with Nos. 24 085 and 25 082 in charge. The site of the halt was almost on the English-Welsh border between Shropshire and Montgomeryshire.

The Main Line Steam Trust 'Welsh Dragon' charter train from Loughborough to Welshpool in June 1973 produced the very unusual sight of a Class 47 on ex-Cambrian metals. Having run round the empty stock, No. 1623 draws the train back towards the down platform to allow passage of a Barmouth to Birmingham DMU service on the up line.

Class 25 No. 25 142 heads an excursion from Brighton to Towyn over the River Severn bridge at Cilciwydd on 27 July 1974. As evidenced by the bridge capacity, the former double track section from Buttington Junction through Welshpool to Forden has now been singled, trains using the former up line across the river.

Nos. 24 134 and 24 036 speed the 09.40 (Saturdays only) Euston to Aberystwyth through Abermule, a station now bereft of all equipment apart from a ground frame controlling up and down home signals and the level crossing gates. The train will shortly run over the site of the disastrous head-on collision which occurred here in January 1921 with fifteen fatalities.

A down train leaving Newtown, on 21 July 1973, with Class 24s Nos. 5146 and 5052 in tandem. Later in the day, returning with the 18.30 Aberystwyth to York mails, No. 5146 disgraced itself by failing at Cemmaes Road and had to be detached before the climb up to Talerddig summit.

The 18.30 mail train from Aberystwyth to Shrewsbury on the climb towards Talerddig summit hauled by Class 24/2 No. 5083 (above) on 12 August and (below) by No. 5062 on 8 June 1972. This and the early morning down turn are the only regular locomotive-hauled passenger trains over the Cambrian line. Note the 4-wheel express parcels vans at the front of the train.

Arrival of the 18.30 Aberystwyth to York mail train at Machynlleth hauled by Class 24/2 No. 5083 on an August Saturday in 1972. Connection is made here with the Cambrian coast line DMU service from Pwhelli.

The only regular locomotive-hauled train over the Cambrian coast line in 1973 was 7 J 16, the 14.06 freight on Tuesdays and Thursdays only, from Portmadoc to Shrewsbury (Coton Hill) seen here arriving at Towyn on 10 May with the inevitable Type 2 Class 24 in charge.

Class 24 No. 5142 comes to a stand in Penrhyndeudraeth station with the daily freight from Portmadoc in order to detach gunpowder vans serving the adjacent explosives works.

The 13.15 Pwhelli-Machynlleth service crosses the 11.54 from Dovey Junction at Portmadoc on the single line Cambrian coast section in June 1973. Apart from occasional excursions and a daily goods service, all trains are worked by DMUs.

Class 24 No. 5142 pulls out of the down sidings at Portmadoc on to the up passing loop with the daily freight to Shrewsbury. The now cleared site of the former Portmadoc steam shed can be seen on the right, May 1973.

An L.N.E.R. Society charter train from Euston to Carmarthen The Central Walesman, on 29 June 1974, hauled by spotlight-fitted Class 37 No. 37 192, passes the lonely station at Llangunllo in Radnorshire, summit of the Central Wales line, 980ft. above sea level. Special excursions such as this are the only locomotive-hauled trains to work between Llandovery and Craven Arms since freight services were withdrawn from the northern section of the line in 1964.

Returning to Euston later in the day by the same route—the 'Central Walesman' hurries through Bucknell between Knighton and Hopton Heath. The signal box, closed as a block post in 1965, has been retained to control the crossing gates over the busy Craven Arms-Knighton road. The 30 or so miles of single track between Craven Arms and Llandrindod Wells is now the longest block section on British Rail.

Shorn of its passing loop but retaining the signal box for protection of the level crossing, Dolau station between Penybont and Llanbister Road on the Central Wales line lapses back into slumber as the 12.02 from Swansea departs towards Shrewsbury, 13 May 1972. The signal box and signals proclaim their L.N.W.R. ancestry. However, the station became an unstaffed halt and ceased to be a block post in 1965.